Engineering
North America's
Landmarks

# Building
the Statue
of Liberty

Laura L. Sullivan

Cavendish
Square
New York

Boulder City Library
701 Adams Boulevard
Boulder City, NV 89005
MAY     2016

D0821681

Published in 2018 by Cavendish Square Publishing, LLC
243 5th Avenue, Suite 136, New York, NY 10016

Copyright © 2018 by Cavendish Square Publishing, LLC

First Edition

No part of this publication may be reproduced, stored in a retrieval system, or transmitted in any form or by any means—electronic, mechanical, photocopying, recording, or otherwise—without the prior permission of the copyright owner. Request for permission should be addressed to Permissions, Cavendish Square Publishing, 243 5th Avenue, Suite 136, New York, NY 10016. Tel (877) 980-4450; fax (877) 980-4454.

Website: cavendishsq.com

This publication represents the opinions and views of the author based on his or her personal experience, knowledge, and research. The information in this book serves as a general guide only. The author and publisher have used their best efforts in preparing this book and disclaim liability rising directly or indirectly from the use and application of this book.

All websites were available and accurate when this book was sent to press.

Library of Congress Cataloging-in-Publication Data

Names: Sullivan, Laura L., 1974- author.
Title: Building the Statue of Liberty / Laura L. Sullivan.
Description: New York : Cavendish Square Publishing, 2018. | Series:
Engineering North America's landmarks | Includes index.
Identifiers: LCCN 2017019387 (print) | LCCN 2017020461 (ebook) | ISBN 9781502629753 (E-book) | ISBN 9781502629722 (pbk.) | ISBN 9781502629746 (library bound) | ISBN 9781502629739 (6 pack)
Subjects: LCSH: Statue of Liberty (New York, N.Y.)--Juvenile literature. | New
York (N.Y.)--Buildings, structures, etc.--Juvenile literature.
Classification: LCC F128.64.L6 (ebook) | LCC F128.64.L6 S85 2018 (print) | DDC 974.7--dc23
LC record available at https://lccn.loc.gov/2017019387

Editorial Director: David McNamara
Editor: Fletcher Doyle
Copy Editor: Rebecca Rohan
Associate Art Director: Amy Greenan
Designer: Alan Sliwinski
Production Coordinator: Karol Szymczuk
Photo Research: J8 Media

The photographs in this book are used by permission and through the courtesy of: Cover, p. 1 Piuxabay. com; p. 4 Matej Hudovernik/Shutterstock.com; pp. 6, 23 Bettman/Getty Images; p. 7 ©iStockphoto. com/ArtemKononenko; p. 9 Archive Holdings Inc./Archive Photos/Getty Images; p. 10 Drmakkoy/ DigitalVision Vectors/Getty Images; p. 12 Library of Congress/Corbis Historical/Getty Images; p. 17 ullstein bild/Getty Images; p. 19 José Miguel Hernández Hernández/Moment/Getty Images; p. 20 FPG/Archive Photos/Getty Images; p. 22 LL/Roger Viollet/Getty Images; p. 25 ©AP Images.

Printed in the United States of America

# Contents

The Statue of Liberty was a gift from France to the United States.

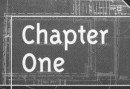

# Chapter One

# Sign of Friendship

After the Union won the Civil War in 1865, slavery was ended. The new United States inspired much of the rest of the world. It represented a love of **liberty**. France really admired the United States.

The monarchy in France ended in the French Revolution (1789–1799). France's motto became *Liberté, Égalité, Fraternité.* This means liberty, equality, and brotherhood. Édouard René de Laboulaye was a French politician and author.

He worked to end slavery. Some time before 1870, he had an idea. He wanted to show French support for the United States. He wished to make the countries better friends. He thought France should build a **colossal** statue as a gift to the United States.

French sculptor Frédéric-Auguste Bartholdi presented the idea of a statue to US politicians.

## A French Idea

He told his idea to a famous French sculptor. Frédéric-Auguste Bartholdi liked the idea. However, he couldn't do the job right away. He already had other projects. Also, France was at war with Prussia (Germany). Finally, Bartholdi crossed the Atlantic Ocean to present the plan in 1871.

He visited many powerful people in New York, including President Ulysses S. Grant. They liked the idea. France agreed to pay for the statue. It would

Liberty Island was formerly known as Bedloe's Island.

**Fast Fact**

The Statue of Liberty's face is said to be modeled on sculptor Frédéric-Auguste Bartholdi's mother, Charlotte Bartholdi. His wife, Jeanne-Emilie, may have been the model for the statue's arms and torso.

build the statue. The United States would give them land for it. It would make a **pedestal** to support it.

## The Perfect Place

The land chosen was on what was called Bedloe's Island. This island is located in Upper New York Bay. It is nearly 15 acres (6 hectares). When Bartholdi docked in New York, the island caught his attention. He saw that all ships coming into New York had to pass that island. It was a perfect location for a giant sculpture. President Grant and

Ships full of travelers and immigrants sailing into New York passed by Liberty Island. This ship arrived in New York Harbor in about 1900.

Congress agreed. The president signed a bill in 1877 making the island the site for the statue. The island was renamed Liberty Island in 1956.

# Statue of Liberty By the Numbers

The Statue of Liberty is located in Upper New York Bay, below Manhattan.

**Fundraising for the statue begins:** 1875

**Time to make the statue:** Eight years, from 1876 to 1884

**Time to assemble the statue:** Four months

**Cost of the statue:** $250,000 each for the statue and the pedestal

**Total height (base of pedestal to torch):** 305 feet 6 inches (93 meters)

**Total weight:** 225 tons (204 metric tons)

**Number of stairs to the crown:** 354

**Shoe size (in US women's sizes):** 879 (average women's shoe size is 8 to 9)

**Number of visitors each year:** 4 million

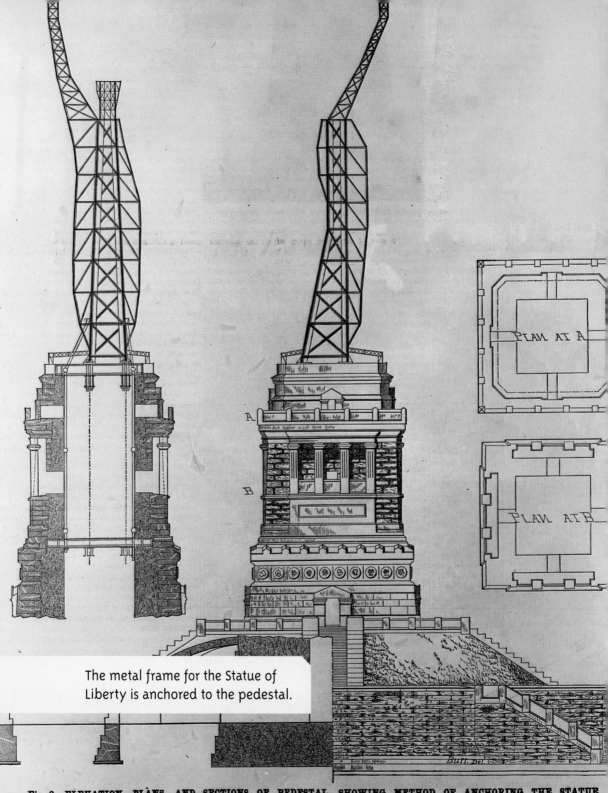

The metal frame for the Statue of Liberty is anchored to the pedestal.

Buff. Del.

Fig. 2.—ELEVATION, PLANS, AND SECTIONS OF PEDESTAL, SHOWING METHOD OF ANCHORING THE STATUE.

Inside the figure: PLAN AT A, PLAN AT B, A, B

# Chapter Two

# Money and Metal

Money was needed to build the Statue of Liberty and its pedestal. It was one of the first projects to ask the public for money. Today, people call it crowdfunding. Some wealthy people made big donations. Everyday citizens donated a lot of the funds. Some were schoolchildren and workers. Thousands of people in France and in the United States gave small amounts of money.

Several American newspapers made a promise. They would print the name of anyone who donated. They would do it even if someone gave only a dime. Many people donated just to see their name in the paper.

## Libertas

Bartholdi had to decide on a design. He wanted a simple design. Small details would be lost on such a huge statue. He decided on a representation

**Fast Fact**

Joseph Pulitzer published the *New York World*. The committee building the pedestal ran out of money in 1884. The *World* ran a story asking everyone to donate money. In five months, 125,000 people gave $100,000. The pedestal was saved.

of a Roman goddess called *Libertas*. In ancient Rome, this goddess was worshiped by many freed slaves. An image of Libertas also appeared on many American coins.

The statue's official name is *Liberty Enlightening the World*. Today, the statue is sometimes called Lady Liberty.

## A Copper Giant

Bartholdi decided the figure would wear robes. It would hold a torch high in the air. The torch is a symbol of enlightenment and progress. It guides people to better things. In her other arm, Lady Liberty holds a tablet. It reads: July IV MDCCLXXVI. Those are the Roman numerals for July 4, 1776. That is the day the United States declared its independence from Britain. She wears a seven-pointed crown. It symbolizes the sun's rays and the seven seas. Bartholdi decided her surface would be made of **copper**.

Bartholdi hired an engineer named Eugène Viollet-le-Duc. They realized a statue made of solid copper would not be strong enough. The engineer came up with a plan to place a thin copper skin over a brick support structure.

## Eiffel Has New Ideas

Unfortunately, Viollet-le-Duc got sick and died in 1879. He didn't leave plans for attaching the copper skin to the supports. The project was in trouble. Then Bartholdi got Gustave Eiffel to join the project. Eiffel later designed the Eiffel Tower in Paris, France.

Gustave Eiffel came up with a way to keep the copper skin from cracking.

There were other problems. One was how to keep the statue from cracking when it moved. Weather changes the statue in many ways. The strong winds in New York Harbor can make the statue sway. A wind of 50 miles per hour (80 kilometers per hour) will move the statue 3 inches (7.5 centimeters). Also, metal parts of the statue expand in the heat and contract in the cold. The designers had to make sure these movements would not crack the copper skin.

## Lady Liberty's Skeleton

Eiffel made the statue's skeleton out of iron. The spine was a strong center **pylon.** It had four feet. It was strengthened by cross braces. It resembles the Eiffel Tower. Eiffel made an iron skeleton around the pylon. It is called the armature. The thin copper skin would be attached to the armature with metal straps linked to an iron mesh. The pylon supported the statue's weight. The weight is called the load. This reduced **stress** on the armature. Having separate internal parts let everything move a tiny bit. This kept the skin from cracking.

The statue was built in pieces. It stayed in Paris until 1885. By then, the pedestal was nearly complete. The Statue of Liberty was taken apart. It was sent to America in a steamship.

# The Curtain Wall

Curtain wall designs are common in buildings with many glass windows.

Eiffel made use of an engineering idea that was new. In most structures, the outside wall is load bearing. That is, it plays a part in supporting the weight of the structure. However, Eiffel saw that this would not work for the Statue of Liberty. Instead, he used **curtain wall** construction. In this method, the supports are all internal. The outside of the building or statue doesn't support any weight. The surface is only for decoration. Today, many modern buildings that have windows covering most of their outside use this design.

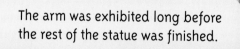
The arm was exhibited long before the rest of the statue was finished.

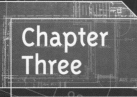

# Chapter Three

# Parts on Display

The Statue of Liberty got a lot of attention before it was put together in New York. The parts were made separately. Sometimes parts went on tour by themselves. The arm, with its huge torch, visited America first. It was part of the Centennial Exhibition in Philadelphia. People could climb up inside the arm to get a bird's-eye view of the fair. The head was completed in 1877. In 1878, it had a starring appearance at the Paris World's Fair.

The Statue of Liberty's head visited the 1878 Paris World Fair.

## Opposition to Lady Liberty

Some people were against the statue before it even came to the United States. The country's economic troubles made it hard to raise money for the pedestal. Some people didn't like that the United States had to pay something for France's gift. Why should we waste our money on the pedestal, some people wondered. Others thought that a US monument should be made by US designers and workers.

The pedestal designers found a way to cut costs. The first design called for a base of solid granite. The second plan was to make most of the base out of concrete. Just the outside could be finished in expensive granite. That would be a lot less expensive.

Emma Lazarus wrote a poem to raise money for the Statue of Liberty. The poem focused on the troubles of immigrants. This plaque is inside the pedestal.

## Huddled Masses Yearning to Breathe Free

Poet Emma Lazarus was asked to write a poem to help raise money for the sculpture. She wrote the famous sonnet titled "The New Colossus." It includes the lines, "give me your tired, your poor, your huddled masses yearning to breathe free ..." However, that poem played no part in the early years of the statue. It wasn't added to a plaque on the pedestal until 1903.

The Statue of Liberty was officially dedicated on October 28, 1886. President Grover Cleveland led

### Fast Fact

Pounding the copper skin into the right shape and thickness was specialized work. Three hundred kinds of hammers were used to shape the metal. They came in all sizes, from huge mallets to tiny hammers.

The Statue of Liberty has had a lot of renovations done to keep it strong and beautiful.

the event. There was a huge parade. Workers at the New York Stock Exchange were so excited that they threw **ticker tape** out the window to make streamers. These were long skinny rolls of paper that showed stock prices. That was New York's first ticker tape parade. The statue soon became famous. It also became a symbol to the many **immigrants** who came to the United States.

## Time Marches On

A few years after it was built, the copper statue started to turn a green-gray color. This is what happens when copper is exposed to air. The color is called **verdigris**. Some people wanted to paint or gild the statue. It was soon decided that the color looked noble and natural.

In the 1980s, the statue was renovated. The arm attachment had weakened and had to be repaired. Also, some of the copper skin was replaced. The torch was covered in gold.

Today, about four million people visit the Statue of Liberty each year. She stands as a symbol of freedom and the ideals of the United States.

# Five Tallest Statues in the US and its Territories

**1. Birth of the New World**  This 360-foot (110 meter) bronze sculpture in Puerto Rico shows Christopher Columbus with his ships behind him.

**2. The Statue of Liberty**  This copper statue stands at 151 feet (46 m) not including the pedestal.

**3. Pegasus and Dragon**  The winged horse fights a dragon in this 100 foot (30 m) sculpture in Hallandale Beach, Florida.

**4. Our Lady of the Rockies**  This Butte, Montana sculpture stands 88.6 feet (27 m) tall.

**5. The Golden Driller**  This 75-foot (23 m) concrete statue of an oil man is in Tulsa, Oklahoma.

# Statue of Liberty Quiz

1. The goddess Libertas, upon which the Statue of Liberty is based, is from what ancient culture?

2. France paid for and built the statue. What part was the United States responsible for?

3. What is the statue's official name?

4. The surface of the Statue of Liberty is made of what metal?

**Answers**

1. Ancient Rome.

2. The pedestal on which the statue stands.

3. *Liberty Enlightening the World.*

4. Copper.

# Glossary

**colossal** So extremely huge it is jaw-dropping.

**copper** A reddish-brown metal that can be shaped.

**curtain wall** An architectural design where the outside of a structure does not support its weight.

**immigrant** A person who comes into a foreign country to live.

**liberty** Having freedom in a society to make decisions without many restrictions.

**pedestal** The support or base on which a statue or monument stands.

**pylon** A pillar-like tower that is used for support.

**stress** The resistance of a material that is being bent or deformed by a load.

**ticker tape** A long spool of thin paper on which stock prices are printed.

**verdigris** The green-gray color that copper turns when exposed to air and sea water.

# ♀ Find Out More

## Books

Holub, Joan. *What Is the Statue of Liberty?* New York, NY: Grosset and Dunlap, 2014.

Malam, John. *You Wouldn't Want to Be a Worker on the Statue of Liberty.* London, UK: Franklin Watts, 2017.

## Websites

**Science Kids: Statue of Liberty**

http://www.sciencekids.co.nz/sciencefacts/engineering/statueofliberty.html

In its engineering section, this website has fun facts about the iconic statue.

**Statue of Liberty National Monument**

https://www.nps.gov/stli/index.htm

This site from the United States National Parks Service has facts about the statue and information on how to visit Lady Liberty.

# Index

Page numbers in **boldface** are illustrations. Entries in **boldface** are glossary terms.

# ♀ About the Author

**Laura L. Sullivan** is the author of more than forty fiction and nonfiction books for children, including the fantasies *Under the Green Hill* and *Guardian of the Green Hill*. She lives in Florida where she likes to swim, hike, canoe, hunt fossils, and practice Brazilian Jiu Jitsu.